Successfully tame budgies within a few weeks. How does clicker training birds with budgerigars work? A step-by-step guide for budgies taming and parakeet training.

By Thorsten Hawk

Content

Taming budgerigars in a few weeks, how does that work?

To own a tame budgerigar is something wonderful and a big wish of many keepers. But how do you get a tame budgie? How long does it take before the bird literally eats out of your hand? And what do you have to pay attention to when taming it? All these questions will be discussed in the next chapters.

But before we start taming, it's worth taking a look at the origin of this sweet little fellow. Knowing where the budgerigar's natural habitat is, and how it moves within it, helps to build up an understanding of appropriate husbandry. In addition, its natural behaviour gives us a few clues to consider when taming it.

The natural habitat of the budgies is the steppe country of Australia. There they live in swarms and follow the water and food sources as nomads. Their greatest enemies are birds of prey and during the breeding season also snakes. Budgies, like all other birds, are rather shy animals and not naturally tame. This natural shyness and possible negative experiences with humans require a lot of patience when taming them. Budgies are often caught and held by previous owners, zoologists or breeders with their bare hands. Their trust in humans is disturbed by this. Despite all these points, the budgie can be tamed with empathy and the right handling.

Can every budgie be tamed?

How tame a budgie can become is partly down to the patience of the owner, and partly to the character of the budgie. Every budgie has its own personality. As with humans, birds can be brave, shy, curious or reserved. Some become tame faster, others need a little longer. It may also have to be accepted that individual animals do not want to establish a relationship with humans and prefer to stay among their conspecifics.

Advantages of a tame budgie

The biggest advantage of a tame budgie is certainly the simplification of the care. When cleaning the cage, the bird does not panic. After the free flight the bird can easily be returned to the cage and a visit to the vet will be much more relaxed with a tame budgie.

The trust and relationship that is built up during taming is a wonderful thing and gives the owner a lot of pleasure. The daily training and the free flights bring the beloved variety for the curious little guys.

Disadvantages of a tame budgie

When the budgie loses its fear, it becomes curious and explores the living space. Thus, a tame budgerigar is more exposed to danger than an untamed one. Hot plates, dangerous objects, forgotten open windows or unhealthy food, on a human plate, become a risk.

How tame can a budgie become? What levels?

There are different kinds of tame. There are different levels that can be reached. For some owners it is enough if the budgie eats out of their hand. Others want the bird to come flying on command or even to be petted.

Patience is one of the key words in taming. If you train regularly and give your bird enough time, you can reach the following levels.

- The budgie eats out of your hand in the cage

- The budgie sits down in the cage on the hand to eat

- The budgie can be taken out of the cage by hand

- After the free flight the budgie can be brought back into the cage on the hand

- The budgie flies to the hand or on the shoulder on command

- Expansion of commands and activities

- The budgie can be gently crawled

It is possible that a tame budgie likes to cuddle. But it is also possible that the owner has to accept that the bird prefers to stay among its conspecifics. The bird should determine where its limit is. No pressure or coercion should be used.

Does gender play a role in taming?

The opinion that male budgies are easier to tame is widespread. However, this cannot be said in general, as owners have had different experiences with taming. Primarily it depends on the character and previous experience of the budgie. One thing is certain, with patience and training females can be tamed as quickly and to the same level as males.

Do only young birds become tame or do old birds also become tame?

Since the young bird has had no or only few bad experiences with humans, it can be said that it is easier to train a young bird. An older bird has a history of possible bad experiences. But with patience an older bird can be tamed.

What to keep in mind for young birds and older birds?

In the case of young birds, the owner can start training as soon as the bird is ready to be fed. It is important that no pressure is exerted on the animal. For example, touching when the bird is not yet ready. These experiences would have a negative effect on the further course of taming. Training should also take place daily, in short units. The bird is overstrained with long units. If the budgie is treated incorrectly or the training is interrupted for several days, this can lead to failure.

An older bird may need more time and the owner must be a little more patient. However, if the same points are observed as for the young bird, it is possible to get the older bird tame.

What do the sounds of budgies tell us?

The body language and the sounds a budgie makes can tell us a lot about the bird's condition.

Chattering songs are the most heard sounds of budgies. It is a gentle melody that can become louder or shrieks from time to time. This singing means that the birds are relaxed and satisfied. If the whole flock is chatting, it can also become louder from time to time. Every bird has its own "voice" and is recognizable by its voice to the other birds, but also to humans.

A screeching budgie does not always have to mean that it is scolding and expressing its displeasure. Sometimes they do this out of overconfidence, to reveal their joy of life.

A two-syllable sound, which is usually sustained and rhythmically emitted, is a contact call. This is usually heard when the budgies are separated or are out of sight in the room. It is noticeable that the second bird picks up the communication and responds. A budgie can also make contact calls to its owner if it does not see him or her or if it is missing.

If the budgie is dissatisfied or feels threatened, he/she expresses this with different sounds. The chirping does not sound cheerful at this point. With growling, hissing, cooing or quickening, the budgie definitely shows that he needs distance. If the budgie feels disturbed, he also expresses this with a snarl. It uses these sounds not only against enemies or humans, but also to warn obtrusive conspecifics.

If the birds are suddenly calm, this can mean danger.

Squeaking or cracking breath sounds can indicate respiratory disease. If such noises can be heard, the bird should be taken quickly to a veterinary surgeon who is familiar with birds.

To clear their airways, budgies may sneeze and cough. It is normal for budgies to do this from time to time. For example, the budgie frees its airways by sneezing before sleeping. If coughing and sneezing occur more frequently during the day or even occur in seizures, the animal should see a doctor.

Dealing with aggressive birds that bite?

The budgerigar's beak plays an important role in the bird's daily life. It is used for feeding and is used as a tool or to feed its partner. They explore unknown things with their tongue and beak. The bird also defends itself with its beak or expresses its affection for its partner and conspecifics by gently biting and crawling.

Once a budgie has gained confidence in its owner, it can show its affection with the same behavior. It explores the skin or hairs with its tongue and beak and nibbles its fingers or hand. The gentle nibbling can also end with a firmer bite. This bite is also called love bite. The bite can be painful, but it is only a sign of the bird's affection and it should never be scared away or even punished.

If the budgie feels threatened, biting is often the only way to get away from the danger. It uses its beak to keep other birds away or to defend its life. Our hand looks threatening to the bird and it will shrink back or possibly go into a threatening position. Budgerigars are escape animals and their enemies are birds of prey, which grab at them with their catches. Our hand reminds the budgerigars strongly of the catches of the birds of prey. This means every budgie has a natural fear of our hand. In order not to frighten the bird unnecessarily, it should not be grasped under any circumstances.

Once a bird has learned that biting has put distance between itself and the threat, this can become a normal habit. This can even lead to the budgie biting when the owner wants to fill up the food or change the water. Breaking this pattern is very difficult. It is therefore important to take precautions and never let it get that far. The animal should always be given its space. Through its defensive posture and defensive sounds, it is easy to see and hear when a bird feels threatened and is getting ready to attack. It is important that the master learns to recognize these first signs of defense. If necessary, he can immediately but slowly withdraw his hand and thus move away from the budgie.

It is important to find out what the reason for the budgie biting is. Only then is the owner able to eliminate the cause. As mentioned above, it can be due to the owner's misconduct. Other reasons for the bite are bad experiences with the previous owner, a mistake in the keeping conditions or an illness.

Possible deficiencies in the keeping can be missing or too short free flights. The budgie needs these free flights to reduce energy. Sufficient free flight can therefore promote a relaxed budgie. Perhaps the bird is also overtired because the night's rest was not long enough or not undisturbed.

If apathy, diarrhea or other symptoms of illness are associated with aggressive behavior, it is possible that the bird is ill and needs medical treatment.

Start of the taming process

The individual weeks should serve as a guideline. Each budgie has its own personality and this affects the training and the training progress. Should it take longer for the budgie to take further steps or is it possibly even faster, this is completely ok.

Preparation of the cage

Before the budgies are bought, it should be made sure that she finds a habitat, which is species-appropriate. An appropriate cage must be constructed with materials that do not endanger the health of the birds. Care should be taken to ensure that the cage is not too full. The budgie should have room for a few flaps of its wings. The number of seats and toys should therefore be kept small. Natural branches belong to the basic equipment of a cage. The claws wear down on the natural wood, which prevents misalignment. Fresh branches with leaves offer a welcome change. Birds love to nibble on them. Therefore, the branches should be non-toxic and unsprayed and must not be picked up at the roadside.

For hygienic reasons, a floor covering is necessary and must be changed regularly. Bird sand, beech wood granulates, hemp litter, cork granulate or bird soil are suitable floor coverings.

Stainless steel bowls ensure good drinking water quality. The water must be changed every day to prevent the formation of germs in the water.

The feed and water points should be easily accessible for the keeper and are therefore placed close to the gate of the cage. This prevents stress during feeding and water changes.

A limestone, a cuttlebone bowl or a bowl with grit should always be provided. The budgie uses this to wipe its beak and it needs the substances for your digestion.

Choosing the location of the cage can be the first step towards successful taming. The budgerigars are positioned at eye level for this. If the location of the cage is too low, the owner will look much bigger than he already is from the birds' perspective. Loud music, conversations or noises from the television can unsettle the budgies. Particularly for acclimatization, a quiet environment should therefore be ensured. Slight background noises are good, as complete silence can make the birds insecure.

Purchase of a pair of budgies. (transport)

The individual keeping of budgies is not allowed. The budgie is a swarm animal and therefore needs at least one conspecific with itself. To work on taming the birds as a pair or in a flock is no disadvantage. Having the birds around gives them security. Some of the animals are more courageous and serve as an example for the others during taming.

For the transport of the budgies, a stable cardboard box is provided by the dealer. These boxes can be used for the transport. A small shoe box is also suitable, which is provided with holes on the side. The lid must be well secured so that the budgies cannot escape. The birds cannot injure themselves in these boxes and are also protected from draughts.

The darkness will calm them down a little and the box can be held directly against the cage so that the birds can climb into their new home. A special transport cage can also be used. But under no circumstances should the budgies be transported in a normal cage. Unknown noises, noise and the incidence of light can frighten the bird so much that it flutters around aimlessly in the cage. This can lead to serious injuries.

The birds will be stressed, so it is important to keep the transport route short. If the budgies are transported in winter, care must be taken that the birds are not hypothermic. A hot water bottle can be used for this purpose, next to the box in a bag. The budgerigar should not be exposed to temperature fluctuations, as it can catch a cold.

The first hours at home

When the budgies have arrived in their new home, the transport box or transport cage can be held to the cage. Under no circumstances should the birds be shooed out of the box. They should climb into their cage by themselves as soon as they are ready.

The new environment and people can be threatening to the birds, which can frighten them. They may sit in a corner and not move. Others climb around wildly looking for an escape route. This behavior is quite normal and as soon as they get used to the environment, they lose this behavior pattern again. It is best to move away from the cage and give the animals a few hours to get used to their new home.

Gain confidence: 1st and 2nd week

Once the budgies have arrived at their new home and have become accustomed to their new environment, the first steps of taming can begin. Creating trust is the motto of the first two weeks.

The activities at the cage should be limited to the most necessary in the first days. When approaching the cage and feeding, you can talk to the birds in a quiet voice. This has a calming effect on the budgies. In addition, the birds get used to the owner's voice already in the early stages of taming. Budgies are able to remember recurring sounds. It can be started early to connect certain words with a certain action. Thus, a foundation-stone is put for later following commands.

Sitting passively in the room helps the birds to get used to people. Reading a book near the cage can be one possibility. No colorful, flashy or red clothes should be worn. The budgies may be afraid of it. Jewelry can also frighten the bird. It is worth taking off the jewelry. The wearing of inconspicuous clothing should be maintained during the further taming steps.

Contact in this phase is only made from outside the cage. The hands are only put into the cage for feeding.

It is a good moment to find out what the budgies like to eat. Pieces of fruit or millet are suitable for this and can be hung on the outside of the cage to see what the budgies like. These delicacies are used as a reward in later training.

In order not to endanger the success of the taming it is important to never catch the budgie with your bare hand. This behavior destroys trust permanently. If one of the birds has to be taken to the vet or transferred, a light tea towel should be placed over it to lift it carefully into the transport box. Gloves can also be an alternative; the budgerigar does not recognize the hand that feeds him. It is of course better if the bird leaves the cage voluntarily, making it easy to transfer it to a transport cage. This is a good reason to continue the training. During the next weeks the budgie will slowly get used to the hand.

Habituation of the hand in the cage: 3rd to 4th week

After the budgies have got used to their new home and the owner, they can now continue taming. The next step is to accustom the animals to the hand. The training sessions should take place daily and should not be too long. The timing of the training should also be considered. Adapting the training to the daily rhythm of the birds will increase the chances of success. During the day the budgerigars are full of energy and react hectically. In the evening hours the birds are usually much calmer and sit relaxed in their place. This is the right moment to work with the animals.

The information is widespread that starving birds become tame faster. The hunger will force the birds to eat out of their hands faster. But this is a method which can put the bird in danger of its life. Depending on their nutritional status, birds can starve to death very quickly. In addition, it is cruelty to animals and it is strictly discouraged.

In the first phase of the training, the millet (or another delicacy) is taken in the hand and held to the grid. Since the budgies already know the millet, they will slowly approach it through the protection of the grid. Soon the chirping friends have realized that there is no danger from the hand and will peck the millet out of the hand.

Once this step has been taken, they can now continue practicing with their hands in the cage. Furthermore, the birds should be spoken to calmly during each training session. The millet, or another delicacy, is clamped between the fingers and the hand is pushed into the cage. The hand should lie motionless in the cage with the outside of the hand pointing upwards. Jerky movements frighten the animals and should be avoided. The birds will be frightened in the first moment. But after a few days the bravest budgie will not be able to resist the treat and will eat the first bite out of his hand. The partner or conspecifics will see the behavior of this bird and will follow its example.

If the budgerigars do not calm down or become panicky, it is important to slowly pull the hand out of the cage. In this case a step back is taken. Feeding from the hand, outside the cage will be trained further. Until the birds react more calmly to the hand.

Touching and hand as seating place: 5th to 6th week

When the budgies are ready to eat out of your hand without fear in the cage, you can start training for the next level. The distance between bird and millet is increased. The bird is out for its treats and will first climb with one leg on the hand, but at the same time it will be on the safe seat with the other. Once the bird is relaxed, the distance can be increased with each training session until the bird moves up with the second leg.

To ask the budgie to climb on the hand, the finger can be pressed gently against the belly of the animal. The outer surface of the hand should always be on top.

If the bird sits on the hand to eat and is relaxed this should be considered a great success and the owner should be proud of himself and his bird. But this does not mean to rest on the success. Now comes the next possible step of taming - the first attempts to take the bird out of the cage on the hand. He will jump off the first few times but at some point, he will remain seated and can be easily taken out of the cage.

From 7 weeks: free flight and return to the cage, dangers in the apartment?

Now the relationship with the owner is strong and full of trust. This is the perfect basis to continue with the training. It is time to train the birds outside the cage.

In the wild, budgies travel many miles in search of food. The birds still have this strong urge to move and want to live it out. Free flight helps the birds to release their excess energy and should be done daily. During free flight, the flight muscles are trained or maintained. In addition, free flight contributes to general well-being and thus to healthy animals.

The first flights should be carried out under supervision. Since the budgerigars can fly freely in the room during this step, all windows and doors must be locked and the room must be made bird-safe. Drawn curtains or blinds prevent the birds from flying into the glass of the window and injuring themselves. Budgies can get trapped in gaps behind cupboards and chests of drawers. These gaps must be secured. Open vessels such as vases or umbrella stands can become a trap. All water sources such as toilets, sinks or aquariums should be secured against drowning. Always turn off heat sources such as irons, candles, smoothing irons or hotplates. Other pets can also become a deadly danger. It is important to check existing indoor plants for toxicity, as budgerigars like to nibble on plants. The same applies to toys. Small parts could be swallowed or ingredients that are harmful to health could harm the bird.

So that the room can be ventilated during free flight it is possible to install a grille. Fly nets are not suitable for this. A wooden frame to which an aviary grille is attached is the right choice.

The budgerigars must not be shooed into the cage after free flight, or even caught by hand. The trust can be disturbed by this and the achieved taming steps are thus destroyed. Therefore, it can happen that the budgies do not spend the first nights in the cage, because they do not go back voluntarily. Budgies are frightened during the night by sounds or dreams and then flutter around uncontrollably. They have poor vision at night and a small light can be helpful for orientation. This can help to ensure that the birds do not injure themselves.

Nightlights, which are also used in children's rooms, are suitable for this.

In order to bring the budgerigars simply back into the cage, a "stick taxi" can be helpful. A stick or a rod serves as a means to bring the budgerigars back into the cage. The treat is attached to one side of the stick and held in place on the other side of the stick. When the birds fly to the treat and land there, they can be carefully brought to the entrance of the cage.

Further taming? On shoulder? Complete apartment?

Daily short training sessions of five to ten minutes are sufficient to continue the training. Long units do not lead to a quick success, because the budgies are no longer receptive after a short time. Pressure is to be avoided in principle. During training it is recommended to pay attention to the bird's body language without interruption. The training is to be stopped when the bird sends appropriate signals.

Budgies can learn to be called on command. An approach on command can be very useful if the free flight is extended to the whole house. In this case, however, it is essential to ensure that all sources of danger in the entire apartment are eliminated.

"Comm" is a short word which is often accepted as a command. You can continue to work with the treat in your hand. Whenever the bird comes to hand, the word "come" is pronounced. The budgerigars connect this word with the treat. After some training sessions the bird knows that a treat is waiting for it when it hears the word "come". He will happily come to pick up his treat.

Once the bird has learned to land on the human hand, the way to the shoulder is not far. There, too, it can help to lure the bird with the treat.

A further, very useful step is the medical and handling training. Here the budgie learns important tricks for the care at home and the visit to the vet. Useful exercises are:

- voluntary walk into the transport cage

- Entering the balance for weight control

- The ingestion of liquid, soft food or medication from a spoon, pipette or syringe

- Touching the foot and letting it lift

Another possibility to train with the budgies is the clicker training. This will be discussed in the next chapter.

Budgies are very intelligent animals and like to be kept busy. The training brings variety into the everyday life of the animals. One possibility to train with the budgies is the clicker training. The clicker training is known from dog training. But it can also be used very well for the training with the budgies.

A clicker is a device which generates a click sound. As an alternative, a ballpoint pen or a tongue clicker can be used. It is important that the sound is short and is only used for clicker training. The advantage of the clicker is that it can be used exactly when the bird has done something right or good. This way he learns that his behavior is correct and that he receives a reward for it. Next time he will know exactly what to do to get the reward.

When training, fun should be the main focus and never work under pressure. It is worthwhile to practice with the birds individually to be able to reward them in a goal-oriented way and to keep the overview.

As a first step of the training the reward is linked to the noise. The animal must learn that the click stands for the "reward". To achieve this, the budgie is rewarded just like that, without any reason. To do this, a treat that the bird likes very much is needed and is only used for training. It must not be a staple food. The moment the bird accepts the treat, i.e. the reward, you click. Over time, the bird will learn that clicking means that it is about to receive a reward.

The next step is to use the target stick. The goal is that the budgie follows this "target stick". You can use a stick, a ballpoint pen or a shashlik skewer as a target stick. The bird should first learn to touch the target stick with its beak and then follow the target stick. Start by holding the target stick in front of the bird. When the bird bites into it, it clicks and a treat is given. Again, do only a few repetitions, then a break is necessary. Usually the budgie understands quickly that he will get something if he bites into the target stick.

If the budgie masters this exercise, the distance between the target stick and the bird is increased. In order to reach the stick, the parakeet must now stretch. Next, the distance is increased so that the bird must move a few steps. Later the distance between the target stick and the bird should be so big that it must fly to the stick to get its reward. Now the budgie can be steered everywhere with the target stick.

The tricks can be extended as far as you like. Even the training of small tricks is possible with the Clicker Training. There is only one thing to consider. The budgie determines its limits and these must be accepted by the owner.

Conclusion

With patient and careful behavior, one can accustom the budgerigars to the human being. It is heartwarming to see how the bird's confidence grows and how it builds an ever-closer relationship with its owner. The goal of the training does not have to be that in the end the budgerigars cuddle with their owner. The budgie is basically not a cuddly toy and every little step towards the owner is positive and should be respected. Budgies are very clever and they will welcome the training sessions to get an occupation in everyday life. The welfare of the animal should always be in the foreground. To work under pressure and compulsion or even with animal-torturing

methods are highly reprehensible and should never be used. With a lot of patience and care the owner will be rewarded for his efforts with a happy and healthy bird. This trusts his master completely and goes with him through thick and thin. This is the most beautiful thing in the world.

Imprint

© 2020 Randy Bolz

Sterndamm 17

12487 Berlin

Edition (1)

Cover design, illustration: Randy Bolz
Editing, proofreading: Randy Bolz
Translation: Kevin Dorrer
Publisher: Randy Bolz
Print: Amazon Europe in Luxemburg

Printed in Great Britain
by Amazon

19454392R00020